Galicia
Travel Guide

Quick Trips Series

No part of this publication may be reproduced, stored in a retrieval system, or transmitted, in any form or by any means without the prior written permission of the publisher, nor be otherwise circulated in any form of binding or cover other than that in which it is published and without similar condition being imposed on the subsequent purchaser. If there are any errors or omissions in copyright acknowledgements the publisher will be pleased to insert the appropriate acknowledgement in any subsequent printing of this publication. Although we have taken all reasonable care in researching this book we make no warranty about the accuracy or completeness of its content and disclaim all liability arising from its use.

Copyright © 2016, Astute Press
All Rights Reserved.

Table of Contents

A CORUÑA, VIGO & COSTA DO MARISCO   5
- Customs & Culture 7
- Geography 9
- Weather & Best Time to Visit 10

SIGHTS & ACTIVITIES: WHAT TO SEE & DO   12
- Santiago de Compostela 12
- A Coruña 17
- Vigo 20
- San Carlos Garden 22
- Monte de San Pedro Park 23
- Galicia Marine Museum 24
- Vigo Municipal Museum 25
- Vigo Zoo 26
- Cies Island & Nature Reserve 27
- Naval Museum and Exponav 28
- Parque Natural Fragas do Eume 30
- Fervenza do Toxa 31
- Illa de Arousa 32
- Aquapark de Cerceda 34

BUDGET TIPS 35

🌐 ACCOMMODATION 35
    La Pensión Palacio..35
    Hostal Riá de Vigo..36
    Pensión Badalada..37
    Hostal Colón Riviera 38
    Hostal J.B..39

🌐 RESTAURANTS, CAFÉS & BARS 40
    Restaurante Boga..40
    O Piorno..41
    Restaurante O Elefante 42
    Restaurante-Raxería El Rubio 43
    Nueva Tapería La Abuela 44

🌐 SHOPPING 45
    Mercado de Abastos de Santiago..45
    C.C. Marineda City..46
    Kailua Kayak (Windsurfing & Kitesurfing) 47
    Fish Auctions 48
    Lacteos Anzuxao 49

KNOW BEFORE YOU GO 51

🌐 ENTRY REQUIREMENTS 51
🌐 HEALTH INSURANCE...51
🌐 TRAVELLING WITH PETS..52
🌐 AIRPORTS...52
🌐 AIRLINES 53
🌐 CURRENCY..54
🌐 BANKING & ATMS 55
🌐 CREDIT CARDS 55
🌐 TOURIST TAXES...56
🌐 RECLAIMING VAT 56

- 🌐 Tipping policy 57
- 🌐 Mobile Phones 57
- 🌐 Dialling Code 58
- 🌐 Emergency Numbers 58
- 🌐 Public Holidays 59
- 🌐 Time Zone 60
- 🌐 Daylight Savings Time 60
- 🌐 School Holidays 60
- 🌐 Trading Hours 61
- 🌐 Driving Laws 61
- 🌐 Drinking Laws 62
- 🌐 Smoking Laws 62
- 🌐 Electricity 63
- 🌐 Food & Drink 63

GALICIA TRAVEL GUIDE

A Coruña, Vigo & Costa do Marisco

Avoid the crowded beaches of the well known costas of Spain and head to the Galician coastline instead for a refreshing and sunny change. In the Costa do Marisco (Shellfish Coast), the Norwegian-style fjords of the Rias Altas hide deserted beaches, shallow lagoons and pretty little villages where freshly caught fish and shellfish are plentiful on local menus.

GALICIA TRAVEL GUIDE

Try the expensive and interesting "percebes" or goose barnacles. The scourge of a sailor's life, these weird looking crustaceans have been eaten for years by the Galician people and are now regarded as a local designer dish.

The densely wooded areas of Galicia hide a wealth of wildlife and in most places the forests and surrounding countryside are unpolluted. The landscapes of the RiasBaixas make this province one of the most beautiful in Spain and get their name from the five flooded valleys in the area. Visitors to the Galician countryside will be puzzled by the many buildings perched on stilts with a cross on the roof. These "horreos" are not religious shrines as many people would imagine but traditional grain stores. They are very rarely used now for their original purpose but are an important part of Galician history and "horreos" souvenirs are available all over the province.

🌐 Customs & Culture

The architecture and culture of the Costa do Marisco dates from Roman times and there are many interesting ruins to see in the cities and all around the province. The Roman Wall of Lugo isthe finest example in western Europe of Roman fortification and is a World Heritage Site.

Contained within the boundaries of the Costa Do Marisco is the Costa da Muerte or coast of death. Stretching from Malpica in the north to Fisterra in the south the treacherous rocks have been responsible for many shipwrecks and loss of life. Fishing is a main income in this area and around 90,000 fishermen catch 50% of Spain's fish.

Being Spain there are enough ferias and fiestas to keep even the most dedicated party lover busy. The biggest is in Santiago de Compostela in July and is the festival of St James the Apostle. Celebrations begin with fireworks in Obradoiro Square on the eve of the Day of the Apostle including the burning of the cathedral façade. The following day offerings are made inside the cathedral to St James and then the parade of giant figures takes to the street.

In October every year 200,000 people make the journey to O Grove for the Fiesta de Exaltación de Marisco. Clams, crab, mussels and fish stew are all on the menu

GALICIA TRAVEL GUIDE

so if you are a fish lover why not plan your trip around this time.

For something a little more dangerous why not go to Laza in Ourense for the OsPeliqueiros Carnival in February/March. The OsPeliqueiros run through the streets waving sticks, the sound of the cowbells on their belts adding to the general noise and cacophony. Wearing outrageous costumes and masks they are allowed to lash out at the crowds who must take the punishment and not hit back.

Wine festivals, flower festivals, history festivals, festivals to celebrate Christopher Columbus and even a festival to cut the tails off wild horses. Yes, it's true, in Pontevedra the horse fair "A Rapa das Bestas" has been turned from a yearly chore into a round of partying. Well, it is Spain after all!

🌍 Geography

On the northwest corner of Spain the Costa de Marisco starts close to A Coruña in the north and finishes south of Vigo near the Spanish-Portuguese border. Facing the Atlantic the coast has been battered over thousands of years by high seas and strong winds and the results can be seen in the intriguing rocky coastline.

A Coruña airport serves the northern part of the coast but the flights are mostly domestic and to the Spanish islands with one international flight to Amsterdam on a seasonal basis. Vigo in the southern part is also mostly domestic with one international destination, Paris. The airport at Santiago de Compostela is the biggest in Galicia and

GALICIA TRAVEL GUIDE

there are more international flights to here as well as domestic ones. A route between the city and London-Gatwick is due to open in June 2013.

There are train stations in all the major towns and cities and direct rail connections across the border into Portugal. An AVE (high speed) station is being constructed in Porto to accommodate the trains that will eventually run on the new line from A Coruña, through Vigo and into Portugal. The line is due to be operational by 2016.

🌍 Weather & Best Time to Visit

The Galician climate is similar to the climate in the Pacific North West of North America with warm, dry summers and mild winters.

GALICIA TRAVEL GUIDE

The area does get rainfall throughout the year and this makes sure the verdant green landscapes remain so. The sometimes-heavy rainfall sweeps in from the Atlantic turning to snow on the higher ground in winter. Vigo has slightly warmer summers and milder winters due to the sheltered location while to the north A Coruña has mild weather but more uniform rainfall through the year.

For anyone that wants to visit Spain in the summer months but doesn't want the heat of the more southern areas the Costa do Marisco and Galicia could be the answer. In July and August the average daily temperature is around 18° C with lows of 15°C and highs of 21.5°c. In winter the average is 14°C dropping down to around 9°C.

The summer weather is still warm enough for sunbathing so light clothing is an essential part of your wardrobe but

GALICIA TRAVEL GUIDE

maybe add a light cardigan or jacket for evenings. An advantage of these lower temperatures means that sightseeing and sleeping are more pleasurable without the hot, sticky heat normally associated with Spain. If you are visiting in the winter months bring a raincoat and umbrella. It might not be that cold but it could be very wet.

GALICIA TRAVEL GUIDE

Sights & Activities: What to See & Do

🌍 Santiago de Compostela

http://www.santiagoturismo.com/

The city of Santiago de Compostela is one end of the

GALICIA TRAVEL GUIDE

European long distance walking route E3, or the Camino de Santiago as the Spanish part is better known.

The 6,950km (4,320) path takes 350 days to complete the whole route and goes through France, Belgium, Luxembourg, Germany, the Czech Republic, Poland, Slovakia, Hungary, along the Black Sea coast into Bulgaria to end at Cape Emine. If you don't have year to spare hiking through Europe a visit to Santiago is still a must do. Santiago is a beautiful city full of history and stunning architecture. Some of the places not to miss are:

Plaza de Obradoiro, the largest square of its kind in Galicia. The plaza takes its name from "Obra de Oro" or work of gold and certainly wasn't named for its colour but maybe for the richness of the buildings on all four sides. They are all of incredible historical interest and are:

GALICIA TRAVEL GUIDE

Santiago Cathedral: A Romanesque structure with Baroque and Gothic additions and one of the most splendid in the country.

The Hospital Real: Founded in 1489 by the Catholic Monarchs, it is now a luxurious parador and is set in four courtyards with a Gothic chapel in the centre dating from 1556.

Palacio de Gelmirez: On the east side is the Archbishop's Palace. A plain looking building which hides the Palacio de Gelmirez, one of the most important secular buildings in Spain. The 30m /100ft long Salòn de Fiestas and Sala des Armas are very popular with tourists as is the second floor medieval kitchen.

GALICIA TRAVEL GUIDE

Palacio de Rajoy: Designed by a Frenchman, Charles Lemaur, the neo-classical building faces the Cathedral. Today it is used as the town hall and parliament building but has in the past been used as a prison.

In the area round the Plaza de Obradoiro are numerous smaller squares, full of interesting buildings and worth investigating. For walking tours of the city an official guide will take you on a two hour walk where you will get a fascinating glimpse into the history behind the old stone walls of Santiago. The tours are in Spanish and/or English and depart from the tourist office. The old town tour is Tuesday and Saturday at 1pm from June to October and Sunday at 1pm for the rest of the year. Prices are €15 per adult and €5 per child. From the tourist office you can book a guided tour of some of the local workshops and see firsthand some of the ancient trading customs of the town: leather, traditional braiding, silverwork and jet stone.

For shopaholics the choice is endless, the three modern shopping centres where you can find all you need under one roof are Área Central' Shopping Centre, As Cancelas and Compostela Shopping Centre. With easy car parking, cinemas, restaurants and play areas for the little ones sometimes this can be the easiest option. Find the Ensanche area in the town centre where tourists and pilgrims rub shoulders with locals going about their daily business.

There are individual shops as well as international names plus a huge selection of bars, cafeterias and restaurants. The best way is just to wander through the streets stopping off for a drink and tapas as the mood takes you.

GALICIA TRAVEL GUIDE

There are several themed markets for a spot of outdoor browsing and the traffic free Salgueiriños market is the biggest general market for clothes and shoes, bed and table linen. There is also a Hippy market selling handmade local crafts, the Cattle market and an Antiques market.

Santiago is home to three hotel and catering colleges and the gastronomy of the city reflects the association of training and good food. The Santiago Gastronomic Guide is an excellent book to learn about local ingredients and where to go and whatto try. Having a long coastline means there are plenty of fishy delights to try and traditionally the best months for fish are months with an "r" in. Galician style octopus is one of the most popular dishes, simply octopus cooked with cayenne pepper and olive oil and for non-fish lovers there is "caldogallego"

GALICIA TRAVEL GUIDE

(Galician stew) made with potatoes and smoked pig fat among other things.

Look out for the "tarta de Santiago" a traditional dessert made with almonds and topped by a layer of icing sugar bearing the Apostle's cross. For cheese lovers the distinct conical shape of the "queso de tetilla" is easy to find and Santiago has many other locally produced cheeses. Galician wines from theRíasBaixas and Ribeira Sacra regions are delicious as is the most well-known wine of the area, Ribiero. Keep the witches and goblins away by finishing off a meal with a queimada or flamed eau-de-vie. The spell that is chanted while this drink is being made from an herb liqueur and other ingredients will keep you safe.

GALICIA TRAVEL GUIDE

 A Coruña

A Coruña sits on a peninsula at the northwest corner of Spain. Hundreds of years ago it was only a tiny strip of land but the buildup of sand due to sea currents has made it into the size it is today.

It was from this isthmus that the ill-fated Spanish Armada departed from in 1588 only to be wiped out by Sir Francis Drake and the British navy. A Coruña is one of only eight cities in the world to have a nearly exact antipodean opposite, in this case Christchurch in New Zealand.

The major part of the town is built on the rocky promontory with the sea crashing on the rocks all around. The promenade, all 13 kilometres of it, runs through the coves, cliff and beaches and right round the headland. While lovers of aqua sports take up surfing, kayaking and

GALICIA TRAVEL GUIDE

sailing the landlubbers stick to walking, cycling and skating round the smooth path and admiring the views.

The Avenida de la Marina by the port with thousands of galleried windows reflecting the light is a spectacular sight. Originally built as houses for fishermen the extra layer of glass was put into keep the rain and spray from getting into the houses. A Coruña is often referred to as Crystal City and there can be amazing light pattern from the sun and reflected in the glass.

The pedestrianised streets are packed with restaurants, tapas bars and shops mixed in with the medieval buildings and squares. When all the hustle and bustle gets too much take a break and visit the beautiful beaches of Orzan and Riazor in the central part of the city opposite the port.

GALICIA TRAVEL GUIDE

To experience some of A Coruñas beautiful architecture and history some of the best places to visit in the town are:

The Tower of Hercules: The 55m/180ft lighthouse is the oldest Roman lighthouse in use today and it is a World Heritage Site and National Monument of Spain.

The Santiago Church: Built in the 12th century and the oldest church in A Coruña.

A Coruña Museum of Fine Arts: From contemporary art to Rodin, from sculpture to paintings, there is lot to see in this museum housed in a beautiful old convent.

The Monte de San Pedro Park and panoramic lift: Stunning views from the top of this very unusual spherical glass lift.

🌐 Vigo

Vigo is one of the major economic and industrial cities in Galicia with the Port of Vigo being the largest in Europe and one of the busiest for sea traffic. With car manufacturing plants, shipyards and all the associated smaller industries the GDP of Galicia is mostly provided by Vigo. Pescanova, the world's largest fishing company has their home here as do many other famous names in the industry. Fish is exported from here to Portugal, Italy, France and as far afield as Asia.

Nowadays tourism is becoming one of the most booming industries in Vigo. Tourists who want to see more than the

GALICIA TRAVEL GUIDE

port, shipyards and car plants won't be disappointed and the Romanesque ruins a few kilometres from the city centre are a good place to start.

Three of the churches in Vigo are extremely important examples of Romanesque architecture in Galicia and are worth visiting.

After the death of Franco in 1975, the 1980's saw a newly liberated Vigo become home to punk and new wave bands. While many of the bands didn't last long a few of the more notorious ones still call Vigo home. A film based on the memories of the Port of Vigo workers losing their jobs was filmed here with the title Los Lunes al Sol (*Mondays In The Sun*).

GALICIA TRAVEL GUIDE

Vigo has more to offer than containers and cruise ships; the sparking, glitzy marina is home to one of the most exclusive yachting clubs in Spain, Real Club Náutico de Vigo. The Casco Vello (old town) is welcoming and everywhere there are bars and restaurants full of Galician people enjoying life. There is a distinct lack of trashy souvenir shops despite the thousands of people that pour into the town off the cruise ships. The locals go about their business and if you want to experience a proper Galician town Vigo will be hard to beat.

For shopping try Casco Vello and La Piedra Market: Higgledy-piggledy streets with tiny shops and the market where you can buy homemade products like cakes, bread and cheese. Príncipe and Urzaiz streets are surrounded by beautiful architecture and there are some of the most fashionable boutiques and famous names in this more modern commercial area.

For a walk in the fresh head for the Celtic Castro ruins. Sandwiched between the leisure parks and nearby forest the Monte de Castro mount has the best views of the city. When the cobwebs have blown away find the Cathedral of Santa Maria which is great for a history lesson and was built between 1816 and 1836 as a replacement for the former Gothic church.

🌐 San Carlos Garden

Paseo del Parrote

15001 A Coruña

Perched high above the town there are some excellent views of the port and San Anton Castle below. The fortress in the park was built in 1843 and is in the old San Carlos bastion. John Moore, an English general who died in battle was laid to rest here and his tomb and bronze bust are both very interesting. These beautiful and romantic gardens are often used for wedding photography.

 Monte de San Pedro Park

A Coruña

The huge expanse of land that has been made into a park for everyone to enjoy used to belong to the Spanish military, the lookout turrets, barracks and underground passageways have been restored and can be explored to give an insight into the life of a soldier. Located high up on the cliffs the soldiers would have an excellent view of any marauding ships trying to enter into the city and the huge

GALICIA TRAVEL GUIDE

cannons still in situ show how seriously the defence of this area was taken. For some light amusement there is a maze with Italian trees and a children's play area.

The park has two distinct attractions; the Cúpula Atlántica, a dome shaped building with 360ª views and the Ascensor (lift) de San Pedro. This spherical glass lift will take you up the cliff side from the car park to the top of the park in just four minutes. A return ticket costs €3. Entry to the park is free and the gates are open from 11am to 8pm in winter and 11am to 10pm in summer.

🌐 Galicia Marine Museum

160 Avenida Atlántida

36208 Vigo

+34 986 247 750

http://museodomar.xunta.es

The museum is in the Punta de Muiño area of Vigo and the buildings that make up the complex are right on the edge of the Atlantic Ocean. The museum is dedicated to the heritage of the sea and there is a lighthouse with spectacular views and an aquarium where the Rias of the Galician system are explained. You can learn about the fishing and preservation methods, old and new, shell fishing and the impact of new technology on the vessels used. The museum is open morning and evening with a break for siesta and the hours vary according to the time of year. The entry fee is €3 for adults and younger children are free.

Vigo Municipal Museum

Parque de Castrelos s/n

36213, Vigo

GALICIA TRAVEL GUIDE

+34 986 295 070

www.museo.devigo.org

Housed in one of Vigo's most beautiful buildings the museum has a fascinating collection of archaeological remains that have be found in the city during excavations and a display of Galician paintings.

The palace housing the museum was built in the 1670's and restoration work was carried out late 19th and early 29th century. Located in Castrelos Park the gardens have fountains and pools and are designed in a French style. The admission is free and the opening times vary from all day to half days and days with siestas. It would be better to check the website or call before visiting.

Vigo Zoo

Plaza de los Leones,

36316, Madroa - Teis,

Vigo

+34 986 267 783

www.vigozoo.com

Vigo Zoo has a wide diversity of trees and plants that blend in well with the surrounding area and covers an area of 55,676 m2. There are around 45 types of birds, 24 mammals, 30 reptiles as well as insects, spiders and butterflies in the enclosures which have been designed with the natural habitat of the animals taken into careful consideration. The Zoo is open all year around but is closed on Mondays except on Bank Holidays, for adults the entrance fee is €5 but there are a wide variety of discounts available.

🌐 Cies Island & Nature Reserve

Vigo

The Cies Islands are a cluster of uninhabited islands that act as a barrier protecting the Rias from violent winds and make a natural safe harbour. There are three main islands; Monte Faro, San Martino and Monteaguada along with the smaller islets of Vinos, O Ruzo, Agoeira and Carabelos. There are many types of flora and fauna living safely on the islands as they were declared a natural park in 1980 and in 2002 became part of the Atlantic Isles Nature Reserve.

The amazing Cíes Islands have the best beach in the world according to a report by The Guardian newspaper in 2007 but if lazing on the white sand looking at the clear, sparkling water gets too boring there are well-defined walking paths and plenty of bird watching. Early evidence shows that the islands were first occupied in the Iron Age and later by the Romans, but constant invasions from the Normans and pirates didn't make for a peaceful existence and in the 1700's the islands were abandoned. A lighthouse was built here in the 19th century but today the only occupants are the game wardens.

There is a small campsite with all the necessary facilities, a shop and a couple of restaurants. Everything, including the menus is in Spanish only so a phrase book might be handy if you are not familiar with the language.

The only access to cover the 14km between Vigo and the largest of the islands is by a 45 minute ferry ride from Vigo, Baiona or Cangas. The ferries run from Easter to September and tickets are strictly limited so booking is advisable. The one vehicle on the island belongs to the park ranger so walking is the only way to get to those deserted coves and beautiful beaches.

🌍 Naval Museum and Exponav

Edificio Herrerías

Cantón Molins

15403, Ferrol

+34 981 336 000

www.exponav.org

The museum has information on all the ships built in the area from 1751 to 1984 along with permanent exhibitions of models, flags, weapons, diving suits and a whole host of other sea related items. Exponav is an exhibition of the history of shipbuilding from the Middle Ages to the present day. Opening times are Tuesday to Friday 9.30am to

GALICIA TRAVEL GUIDE

1.30pm and weekends and holidays from 10.30am to 1.30pm.

Ferrol has two claims to fame; in the 17th century it was the biggest military arsenal in Europe and in 1892 it was the birthplace of General Francisco Franco. Ferrol town centre takes its inspiration from Lisbon in Portugal and is basically a rectangle with two squares on either side and six parallel streets that are home to the best galleries, shops, bars and restaurants.

Ferrol is very much a Spanish working town but there are some beautiful beaches north of the town and the Castillo de San Felipe is worth visiting.

… **GALICIA TRAVEL GUIDE**

🌐 Parque Natural Fragas do Eume

Oficina del Parque Natural de Fragas do Eume

Lugar de Esteiro 23, 15600

+34 981495580

www.viveaonatural.xunta.es/

The park covers an area of some 9,000 square hectares and is covered with a wide variety of trees, from cork trees growing on the sunny south side to lichens and moss clinging onto the damp north facing rocks. The natural park is full of lush vegetation with some wonderful walks through the fairy tale woods dappled with shade from the canopy of oak trees. Close to the Pontedeume side of the park is an old monastery and there is a free bus service in high season if you don't wish to walk. After travelling hundreds of kilometres the river Eume wriggles through the oaks in the forest before spilling out into an estuary and the sea.

In the town of Pontedeume there is a visitor centre at the park entrance although there are four other points of entry around the perimeter allowing access to the different areas. You can get details of the park at the visitor centre and information about the set walking trails of different levels. The park was subject to fire in March 2012 and some of the more important areas were affected but not the monastery or the homes of the 500 people who live in the park.

❂ Fervenza do Toxa

Located between Silleda and Merza

Pontevedra

GALICIA TRAVEL GUIDE

For hiking, waterfalls and nature take a trip to the Fervenza La Toja just north of Silleda, Pontevedra. The Tojariver pours over the rocks from a height of 60 metres creating a spectacular waterfall in the midst of a beautiful green landscape. Picnic benches and seats directly opposite the tumbling waters offer a welcome place to rest after a walk through the woods. If you visit in the summer months take a swimming costume and towels as there are tranquil pools where you can stop for a cooling dip.

Look out for fauna that is mostly associated with rivers. Badgers, otters and weasels can often be seen along with many trout splashing about in the clear waters while peregrine falcons fly overhead.

GALICIA TRAVEL GUIDE

🌐 Illa de Arousa

Pontevedra

http://www.ailladearousa.com

Connected to the mainland by a two-kilometre bridge is the Illa de Arousa. In the census 2011 around 5,000 people lived on the tiny seven square kilometre island which is the only island municipality in Galicia.

Measuring about four km from one end to the other there are several neighbourhoods and one church. The lighthouse at Cabalo Point stands tall on the granite rocks keeping guard over the rocks and beaches scattered along the coastline. The narrowest point of the island is a mere 200 metres wide and passing through the houses on this tiny strip makes you wonder about high tide.

The far side of the island is more open and it is worth the walk to see the weirdly shaped rocks and keep a look out for the one shaped like a Gremlin. If you decide to walk to take advantage of the views from the lighthouse then end your trip at the bar where you can enjoy a refreshing drink. In the main part of the town the harbor is home to hundreds of little fishing boats gently bobbing up and down at anchor in the bays and moored up at the many jetties.

Needless to say there are of course bars and restaurants for you enjoy freshly caught fish, prepared Galician style of course.

🌎 Aquapark de Cerceda

Polígono do Acevedo s/n

15185 Cerceda - A Coruña

GALICIA TRAVEL GUIDE

+ 34 981 685 036

http://www.aquapark.cerceda.org

Aquapark de Cerceda is the only park of its kind in Galicia and while it might not be the biggest waterpark in the world there is more than enough to keep the family amused for a day out.

There are plenty of pools of all shapes and sizes along with a wave pool, roller coaster ride, aquatubo, kamikaze and slides of varying lengths. There is a playpark for the little ones, a caféteria and plenty of space to sunbathe with lockers, sunbeds and umbrellas for hire. The park is open for the summer months from mid-June to mid-September from 10 noon to 8pm. Adult prices are €7 weekdays and €8 at the weekends, while children pay €5 weekdays and €6 at the weekends.

GALICIA TRAVEL GUIDE

Budget Tips

🌍 Accommodation

La Pensión Palacio

Plaza de Galicia, Nº2, 4ºD

15004

La Coruña

+34 981 122 338

GALICIA TRAVEL GUIDE

La Pensión de Palacio has been open for more than 50 years and is owned and run by Manolo and Flora.

Ideally located in the beautiful Plaza de Galicia the Pensión welcomes guests for both long and short stays, as well as students. There is a restaurant, a laundry service plus parking and garage spaces available. If you want to bring your pet with you, he or she will be more than welcome.

Everything you could need is within 100 metres of your accommodation including bars, shops, restaurants, supermarkets and chemists. Another couple of hundred metres or so further and you will find some of the most attractive and important parks in La Coruña. Room prices are reasonable at €19 for a single, €28 for a double and

€38 for a triple room. All the rooms have washbasins but the other facilities are shared.

Hostal Riá de Vigo

Rúa de Cervantes, 14

36201, Vigo

+34 986 437 240

www.hostalriadevigo.com

The hostal is in the centre of Vigo and with only ten rooms you will be treated like one of the family during your stay. The sea is only a few steps away and in the Old Town nearby you will find plenty of artisan craft shops. There is plenty going on in the surrounding area with museums, theatres, cultural centres and of course there are lots of restaurants where you can try some delicious fish dishes or typical Galician cuisine.

There are single, double and triple bedded rooms to choose from and all the rooms have private bathrooms, heating, television and Wifi. There are rooms available for smokers and pets are accepted. Single rooms cost €20, double €25 / €30 and triple €45 and €55.

Pensión Badalada

Rúa Xelmírez 30, 15704

Santiago de Compostela

+34 981 572 618

www.badalada.es

Pensión Badalada is on a slight incline in the maze of streets surrounding the Cathedral and you can wake to the sound of the bells in the morning. The pension opened in 2008 and is in an antique house that has been tastefully restored with local stone and wood to create an intimate atmosphere.

The rooms are beautifully decorated and have private bathrooms. The communal areas are warm and welcoming and the staff are very friendly and will do their utmost to help you. For anyone wanting to walk the Camino de Santiago there is a luggage storage room to leave your belongings in for a small fee. Room prices are from €35 for a single room and €49 for a double.

Hostal Colón Riviera

Rúa Cristóbal Colón nº 29

Santa Eugenia de Riviera

+ 34 981 870 415

www.hostalcolonriveira.com/

GALICIA TRAVEL GUIDE

This two star hostel is a stone's throw from the seafront and offers comfortable accommodation in a family run business that opened in 1988. A few metres away is the local church and all the historical and cultural sights that the town has to offer.

There is a fully stocked bar and breakfast is available in the wood panelled restaurant. The 22 rooms have private bathrooms, television, central heating, hairdryers and free Wifi. Cots and irons are available on request free of charge. Individual rooms are priced from €24 and double rooms from €30.

Hostal J.B.

Rúa Playa, 3

Malpica De Bergantiños

15113 La Coruña

GALICIA TRAVEL GUIDE

Teléfono: 981 721 906

www.hostaljb.es

Hostal J.B. is 52km from the capital of A Coruña and is set in a super location. The little town has the harbor on one side and a beautiful curving sandy beach on the other.

The hostel is situated on the seafront and is ideal for a tranquil stay on this wonderful part of Spain. The rooms all have private bathroom, television and heating. There is a lift and free Wifi. Some of the rooms have terraces with a sea view. A double room is priced from €30 and a single room from €20.

🌐 Restaurants, Cafés & Bars

Restaurante Boga

Concepcion Arenal 7,

36201Vigo,

+34 886 125 854

A small café-bar that is a great place for a drink or a light meal. In the warmer months the tables outside are ideal to sit and watch the locals going about their business. The beer is well priced and comes with free tapas. There is a good selection of wines to go with the menu of seafood, tapas and typical Spanish dishes. Expect to pay somewhere between €11to €26 for a meal.

GALICIA TRAVEL GUIDE

O Piorno

Rua Caldeira, 24,

Santiago de Compostela,

+34 881 259 002

www.opiorno.com

The old building that houses O Piorno used to be a haberdashery and care has been taken to try and keep some of the atmosphere of years gone by. The restaurant is bright and modern but still retains a certain charm and the portions are large and the staff friendly and attentive. One of the house specialties is octopus weighing around 1.5kg cooked with olive oil, sweet and spicy pepper. The prices range from €13 to €26.

GALICIA TRAVEL GUIDE

Restaurante O Elefante

Azibechería, 5 (Zona Vella)

15704, Santiago de Compostela

+34 902 091 466 ext. 8776

O Elefante is a vegetarian restaurant with a menu full of surprises with not just well known dishes but homemade creations that include their own brand of veggie nut burger. They also serve a wonderful range of healthy drinks and milk shakes and have homemade vegetarian desserts. Only a few steps from the Cathedral at night the restaurant becomes alive with the addition of cocktails. There is a terrace, access for disabled guests and pets are welcome outside.

GALICIA TRAVEL GUIDE

Open Monday, Wednesday and Sunday from 9am to 1.30am, Thursday, Friday and Saturday from 9am to 3.30am. Closed Tuesdays. To find the restaurant head for Plaza de Cervantes, look for the Azibecheria Museum and O Elefante is in one of the narrow streets close by.

Restaurante-Raxería El Rubio

Hersa, 8

Culleredo,

15670, A Coruña

+34 657 551 882

Raxeria El Rubio is located in a pedestrian street and serves traditional Gallegan cooking. They serve tapas, meals and a special menú El Rubio. Their specialties are Raxa and Zorza which are pork loin dishes cooked in two different ways. For fish lovers try the bacalao a la nata (cod in cream) or the unmistakable flavours of freshly cooked trout. For families there is a children's menu as well as a garden area with play equipment. There is disabled access and free Wifi. El Rubio is open every day apart from Tuesday from 10am to close. The daily menu is good value at less than €15 and there is an á la carte menu if you prefer to choose something different.

Nueva Tapería La Abuela

San Lorenzo, 22

Baiona, 36300

Pontevedra

+34 902 091 466 ext.8819

The old medieval town of Baiona has much to offer and situated a few streets from the harbour and the Convento de Dominicas is Tapería La Abuela. More of a snack bar than a restaurant they offer pizzas, burgers, snack and sandwiches and a menu of the day. On Mondays there is a special offer of a drink and tapas for only €1, at other times the prices are still great and most items including the daily menu are less than €15. Open seven days a week from 9am to 2am.

🌐 Shopping

Mercado de Abastos de Santiago

Rúa das Ameas,

15704 Santiago de Compostela

34 981 58 34 38

http://www.mercadodeabastosdesantiago.com/

The original building that housed the market was demolished in 1937 making room for the current one that opened in 1941.

GALICIA TRAVEL GUIDE

The high curved ceiling of the fresh food market has many arched windows flooding the hustle and bustle with light. The old Spanish señoras dressed in black crowd round the stalls and select the best produce, shouting at the stall owners for attention.

There are all types of goods available from fruit to fowl and fish, bakeries, butchers and bookshops, flowers and frozen food, clothes and key cutting.

An innovative market, you can take your fresh produce to the bar outside and for a few euros have it cooked while you wait. Fresh milk is available from a vending machine, bring your own bottles or buy on site. The market is open from Monday to Saturday from 7am to 3pm.

GALICIA TRAVEL GUIDE

C.C. Marineda City

Carretera de Baños de Arteixo, N 43

15008, A Coruña

+34 881 888 888

www.marinedacity.es

This is a mega-shopping centre with something for all the family. There is a cinema, a bowling alley, a brilliant kids zone and a karting track plus an arcade for the over 18's. The children are cared for by the qualified staff while parents wander round the shops or have a peaceful lunch on the restaurant floor lined with palm trees under the glass roof.

There is a huge variety of shops spread over the three floors with fashion, shoes, beauty, furniture, sports goods,

GALICIA TRAVEL GUIDE

electrical and much more from internationally known shops. There are also shops selling locally produced crafts and crafts from Galicia and northeast Spain. The shopping centre is open Monday to Saturday from 10am to 10 pm and the restaurants and leisure activities are open from Sunday to Thursday from 12 noon until midnight and Fridays, Saturdays and fiesta days from 12 noon to 1am. The arcade is open from 12 noon until 11pm.

Kailua Kayak (Windsurfing & Kitesurfing)

Ruá Escultor Gregorio Fernández, 14

36204 Vigo

+ 34 986 227 533

www.kailuakayak.es

GALICIA TRAVEL GUIDE

For water sports enthusiasts there cannot be a better place to go. The 300m2 shop has everything you could need and more for spending thrilling days both on and in the water. Whether you are looking for a small item to make your kit complete or are a beginner wanting advice and all the necessary equipment, the staff at Kailua Kayak are friendly, knowledgeable and attentive. They hold open days where equipment can be tried out to see if you are choosing the right sport and the shop even has its own Kailua windsurf team. There is a huge selection of kayaks, canoes, boards and sails and clothing, wetsuits, helmets as well, plus some really good discounts on secondhand equipment.

Fish Auctions

Any of the fishing harbours will have fish auctions and it a brilliant way to see how the fishermen sell their catch and

GALICIA TRAVEL GUIDE

how the restaurants and shops haggle for the best price. The "nasas" (fishing baskets) are set the previous day and when the fishing boats return to harbour the fish is auctioned off, usually in the afternoon. Lobsters and crabs are always found at the afternoon auctions as are clams, goose barnacles and cockles which depend on the tidal conditions. May, June, July and August are classed as the "closed" season for shellfish so if you are after crabs and clams perhaps time your visit for the winter months.

If you don't fancy braving the quayside try the busy fish markets of San Augustin and Santa Lucia in A Coruña, or the Municipal Market in Pontevedra and for something smaller the local market at Bueu, close to Vigo. Nearly every coastal town will have a fish market and once you have seen the shiny bodies of the freshly caught fish and caught the tang of the sea you will be off to the nearest restaurant to try some of these wonderful delights.

Lacteos Anzuxao

Madriñan, 2

36512 Lalin

Pontevedra

+34 986 794 135

www.lacteosanzuxao.com

In the Deza region is the Pazo de Anzuxao, a fantastic example of local architecture which dates back to 1713 and has been beautifully preserved. For more than forty years the dairy farm here has produced cheeses using traditional Galician methods but before you enjoy the cheeses go for a wander in the peaceful gardens. A team of about a dozen people work at the dairy and produce

GALICIA TRAVEL GUIDE

the famous cone-shaped "tetilla" under their own name ofArzúa-Ulloa, as well as curd cheese, hard, cured cheese and low fat cheeses with semi-skimmed milk. The various processes can be seen and samples tasted with full sized versions available to purchase.

Know Before You Go

🌐 Entry Requirements

By virtue of the Schengen agreement, visitors from other countries in the European Union will not need a visa when visiting Spain. Additionally visitors from Switzerland, Norway, Lichtenstein, Iceland, Canada, the United Kingdom, Australia and the USA are also exempt. Independently travelling minors will need to carry written permission from their parents. If visiting from a country where you require a visa to enter Spain, you will also need to state the purpose of your visit and provide proof that you have financial means to support yourself for the duration of your stay. Unless you are an EU national, your passport should be valid for at least 3 months after the end of your stay.

🌐 Health Insurance

Citizens of other EU countries are covered for emergency health care in Spain. UK residents, as well as visitors from Switzerland are covered by the European Health Insurance Card (EHIC), which can be applied for free of charge. Visitors from non-Schengen countries will need to show proof of private health insurance that is valid for the duration of their stay in Spain, as part of their visa application.

GALICIA TRAVEL GUIDE

🌐 Travelling with Pets

Spain participates in the Pet Travel Scheme (PETS) which allows UK residents to travel with their pets without requiring quarantine upon re-entry. Certain conditions will need to be met. The animal will have to be microchipped and up to date on rabies vaccinations. Additionally, you will need a PETS re-entry certificate issued by a UK vet, an Export Health Certificate (this is required by the Spanish authorities), an official Certificate of Treatment against dangerous parasites such as tapeworm and ticks and an official Declaration that your pet has not left the qualifying countries within this period. Pets from the USA or Canada may be brought in under the conditions of a non-commercial import. For this, your pet will also need to be microchipped (or marked with an identifying tattoo) and up to date on rabies vaccinations.

🌐 Airports

Adolfo Suárez Madrid–Barajas Airport (MAD) is the largest and busiest airport in Spain. It is located about 9km from the financial district of Madrid, the capital. The busiest route is the so-called "Puente Aéreo" or "air bridge", which connects Madrid with Barcelona. The second busiest airport in Spain is **Barcelona–El Prat Airport** (BCN), located about 14km southwest from the center of Barcelona. There are two terminals. The newer Terminal 1 handles the bulk of its traffic, while the older Terminal 2 is used by budget airlines such as EasyJet.

Palma de Mallorca Airport (PMI) is the third largest airport in Spain and one of its busiest in the summer time. It has the capacity of processing 25 million passengers annually. **Gran Canaria Airport** (LPA) handles around 10 million passengers annually and connects travellers with the Canary Islands. **Pablo Ruiz Picasso Malaga Airport** (AGP) provides access to the Costa del Sol. Other southern airports are **Seville Airport** (SVQ), **Jaen Federico Garcia Lorca Airport** (GRX) near Granada, **Jerez de la Frontera Airport**, which connects travellers to Costa del Luz and Cadiz and **Almeria Airport** (LEI).

Airlines

Iberia is the flag carrying national airline of Spain. Since a merger in 2010 with British Airways, it is part of the International Airlines Group (IAG). Iberia is in partnership with the regional carrier Air Nostrum and Iberia Express, which focusses on medium and short haul routes. Vueling is a low-cost Spanish airline with connections to over 100 destinations. In partnership with MTV, it also provides a seasonal connection to Ibiza. Volotea is a budget airline based in Barcelona, which mainly flies to European destinations. Air Europe, the third

GALICIA TRAVEL GUIDE

largest airline after Iberia and Vueling connects Europe to resorts in the Canaries and the Balearic Islands and also flies to North and South America. Swiftair flies mainly to destinations in Europe, North Africa and the Middle East.

Barcelona-El Prat Airport serves as a primary hub for Iberia Regional. It is also a hub for Vueling. Additionally it functions as a regional hub for Ryanair. Air Europe's primary hubs are at Palma de Mallorca Airport and Madrid Barajas Airport, but other bases are at Barcelona Airport and Tenerife South Airport. Air Nostrum is served by hubs at Barcelona Airport, Madrid Barajas Airport and Valencia Airport. Gran Canaria Airport is the hub for the regional airline, Binter Canarias.

🌐 Currency

Spain's currency is the Euro. It is issued in notes in denominations of €500, €200, €100, €50, €20, €10 and €5. Coins are issued in denominations of €2, €1, 50c, 20c, 10c, 5c, 2c and 1c.

🌐 Banking & ATMs

You should have no trouble making withdrawals in Spain if your ATM card is compatible with the MasterCard/Cirrus or Visa/Plus networks. If you want to save money, avoid using the dynamic currency conversion (DCC) system, which promises to charge you in your own currency for the Euros you withdraw. The fine print is that your rate will be less favorable. Whenever possible, opt to conduct your transaction in Euros instead. Do remember to advise your bank or credit card company of your travel plans before leaving.

🌐 Credit Cards

Visa and MasterCard will be accepted at most outlets that handle credit cards in Spain, but you may find that your American Express card is not as welcome at all establishments. While shops may still be able to accept transactions with older magnetic strip cards, you will need a PIN enabled card for transactions at automatic vendors such as ticket sellers. Do not be offended when asked to show proof of ID when paying by credit card. It is common practice in Spain and Spaniards are required by law to carry identification on them at all times.

🌐 Tourist Taxes

In the region of Catalonia, which includes Barcelona, a tourist tax of between €0.45 and €2.50 per night is levied for the first seven days of your stay. The amount depends on the standard of the establishment, but includes youth hostels, campgrounds, holiday apartments and cruise ships with a stay that exceeds 12 hours.

GALICIA TRAVEL GUIDE

🌏 Reclaiming VAT

If you are not from the European Union, you can claim back VAT (or Value Added Tax) paid on your purchases in Spain. The VAT rate in Spain is 18 percent. VAT refunds are made on purchases of €90.15 and over from a single shop. Look for shops displaying Global Blue Tax Free Shopping signage. You will be required to fill in a form at the shop, which must then be stamped at the Customs office at the airport. Customs officers will want to inspect your purchases to make sure that they are sealed and unused. Once this is done, you will be able to claim your refund from the Refund Office at the airport. Alternately, you can mail the form to Global Blue once you get home for a refund on your credit card.

🌏 Tipping policy

In general, Spain does not really have much of a tipping culture and the Spanish are not huge tippers themselves. When in a restaurant, check your bill to see whether a gratuity is already included. If not, the acceptable amount will depend on the size of the meal, the prestige of the restaurant and the time of day. For a quick coffee, you can simply round the amount off. For lunch in a modest establishment, opt for 5 percent or one euro per person. The recommended tip for dinner would be more generous, usually somewhere between 7 and 10 percent. This will depend on the type of establishment.

In hotels, if there is someone to help you with your luggage, a tip of 1 euro should be sufficient. At railway stations and airports, a tip is not really expected. Rounding off the amount of the fare to the nearest euro would be sufficient for a taxi driver. If you recruited a private driver, you may wish to tip that person at the end of your association with him.

🌍 Mobile Phones

Most EU countries, including Spain uses the GSM mobile service. This means that most UK phones and some US and Canadian phones and mobile devices will work in Spain. While you could check with your service provider about coverage before you leave, using your own service in roaming mode will involve additional costs. The alternative is to purchase a Spanish SIM card to use during your stay in Spain.

Spain has four mobile networks. They are Movistar, Vodafone, Orange and Yoiga. Buying a Spanish SIM card is relatively simple and inexpensive. By law, you will be required to show some form of identification such as a passport. A basic SIM card from Vodafone costs €5. There are two tourist packages available for €15, which offers a combination of 1Gb data, together with local and international call time. Alternately, a data only package can also be bought for €15. From Orange, you can get a SIM card for free, with a minimum top-up purchase of €10. A tourist SIM with a combination of data and voice calls can be bought for €15. Movistar offers a start-up deal of €10. At their sub-branches, Tuenti, you can also get a free SIM, but the catch is that you need to choose a package to get it. The start-up cost at Yoiga is €20.

Dialling Code

The international dialling code for Spain is +34.

Emergency Numbers

All Emergencies: 112 (no area code required)

Police (municipal): 092

Police (national): 091

Police (tourist police, Madrid): 91 548 85 37

Police (tourist police, Barcelona): 93 290 33 27

Ambulance: 061 or 112

Fire: 080 or 112

Traffic: 900 123 505

Electricity: 900 248 248

Immigration: 900 150 000

MasterCard: 900 958 973

Visa: 900 99 1124

GALICIA TRAVEL GUIDE

🌐 Public Holidays

1 January: New Year's Day (Año Nuevo)

6 January: Day of the Epiphany/Three Kings Day (Reyes Mago)

March/April: Good Friday

1 May: Labor Day (Día del Trabajo)

15 August: Assumption of Mary (Asunción de la Virgen)

12 October: National Day of Spain/Columbus Day (Fiesta Nacional de España or Día de la Hispanidad)

1 November: All Saints Day (Fiesta de Todos los Santos)

6 December: Spanish Constitution Day (Día de la Constitución)

8 December: Immaculate Conception (La Immaculada)

25 December: Christmas (Navidad)

Easter Monday is celebrated in the Basque region, Castile-La Mancha, Catalonia, La Rioja, Navarra and Valencia. 26 December is celebrated as Saint Stephen's Day in Catalonia and the Balearic Islands.

🌐 Time Zone

Spain falls in the Central European Time Zone. This can be calculated as Greenwich Mean Time/Co-ordinated Universal Time (GMT/UTC) +2; Eastern Standard Time (North America) -6; Pacific Standard Time (North America) -9.

GALICIA TRAVEL GUIDE

🌐 Daylight Savings Time

Clocks are set forward one hour on the last Sunday in March and set back one hour on the last Sunday in October for Daylight Savings Time.

🌐 School Holidays

Spain's academic year is from mid-September to mid-June. It is divided into three terms with two short breaks of about two weeks around Christmas and Easter.

🌐 Trading Hours

Trading hours in Spain usually run from 9.30am to 1.30pm and from 4.30pm to 8pm, from Mondays to Saturdays. Malls and shopping centers often trade from 10am to 9pm without closing. During the peak holiday seasons, shops could stay open until 10pm. Lunch is usually served between 1pm and 3.30pm while dinner is served from 8.30 to 11pm.

🌐 Driving Laws

The Spanish drive on the right hand side of the road. You will need a driver's licence which is valid in the EC to be able to hire a car in Spain. The legal driving age is 18, but most rental companies will require you to be at least 21 to be able to rent a car. You will need to carry your insurance documentation and rental contract with you at all times, when driving. The speed limit in Spain is 120km per hour on motorways, 100km per hour on dual carriageways and 90km per hour on single carriageways. Bear in mind that it is illegal to drive in Spain wearing sandals or flip-flops.

You may drive a non-Spanish vehicle in Spain provided that it is considered roadworthy in the country where it is registered. As a UK resident, you will be able to drive a vehicle registered in the UK in Spain for up to six months, provided that your liabilities as a UK motorist, such as MOT, road tax and insurance are up to date for the entire period of your stay. The legal limit in Spain is 0.05, but for new drivers who have had their licence for less than two years, it is 0.03.

🌐 Drinking Laws

In Spain, the minimum drinking age is 18. Drinking in public places is forbidden and can be punished with a spot fine. In areas where binge drinking can be a problem, alcohol trading hours are often limited.

🌐 Smoking Laws

In the beginning of 2006, Spain implemented a policy banning smoking from all public and private work places. This includes schools, libraries, museums, stadiums, hospitals, cinemas, theatres and shopping centers as well as public transport. From 2011, smoking was also banned in restaurants and bars, although designated smoking areas can be created provided they are enclosed and well ventilated. Additionally tobacco products may only be sold from tobacconists and bars and restaurants where smoking is permitted. Smoking near children's parks, schools or health centers carries a €600 fine.

🌐 Electricity

Electricity: 220 volts

Frequency: 50 Hz

Your electrical appliances from the UK and Ireland should be able to function sufficiently in Spain, but since Spain uses 2 pin sockets, you will need a C/F adapter to convert the plug from 3 to 2-pins. The voltage and frequency is compatible with UK appliances. If travelling from the USA, you will need a converter or step-down transformer to convert your appliances to 110 volts. The latest models of many laptops, camcorders, cell phones and digital cameras are dual-voltage with a built in converter.

GALICIA TRAVEL GUIDE

🌐 Food & Drink

Spanish cuisine is heavily influenced by a Moorish past. Staple dishes include the rice dish, Paella, Jamon Serrano (or Spanish ham), Gazpacho (cold tomato-based vegetable soup), roast suckling pig, chorizo (spicy sausage) and the Spanish omelette. Tapas (hot or cold snacks) are served with drinks in Spanish bars.

The most quintessentially Spanish drink is sangria, but a popular alternative with the locals is tinto de verano, or summer wine, a mix of red wine and lemonade. Vino Tinto or red wine compliments most meal choices. The preferred red grape type is Tempranillo, for which the regions of Roija and Ribera del Duero are famous. A well-known sparkling wine, Cava, is grown in Catalonia. Do try the Rebujito, a Seville style mix of sherry, sparkling water and mint. The most popular local beers are Cruzcampo, Alhambra and Estrello Damm. Coffee is also popular with Spaniards, who prefer Café con leche (espresso with milk).

Websites

http://www.idealspain.com
A detailed resource that includes legal information for anyone planning a longer stay or residency in Spain.
http://spainattractions.es/

GALICIA TRAVEL GUIDE

http://www.tourspain.org/

http://spainguides.com/

http://www.travelinginspain.com/

http://wikitravel.org/en/Spain

Printed in Great Britain
by Amazon